TRAUMATIC BRAIN INJURY
FROM CONCUSSION TO COMA

CONNIE GOLDSMITH

TWENTY-FIRST CENTURY BOOKS / MINNEAPOLIS

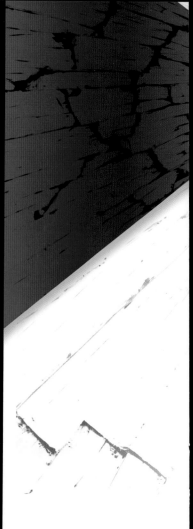

The information about concussion symptoms and diagnosis found in this book is not a substitute for a consultation with a trained medical professional. The author and publisher disclaim responsibility for any adverse effects from information found here. If you think you may have suffered a concussion, consult a doctor immediately.

The author dedicates this book to veterans of the Iraq and Afghanistan wars who sustained traumatic brain injuries, and to the families, friends, and medical professionals who care for them.

Twenty-First Century Books
A division of Lerner Publishing Group, Inc.
241 First Avenue North
Minneapolis, MN 55401 U.S.A.

For reading levels and more information, look up this title at www.lernerbooks.com.

Library of Congress Cataloging-in-Publication Data

Goldsmith, Connie, 1945–
        Traumatic brain injury : from concussion to coma / by Connie Goldsmith.
            pages   cm
        Includes bibliographical references and index.
        ISBN 978–1–4677–1348–1 (lib. bdg. : alk. paper)
        ISBN 978–1–4677–2550–7 (eBook)
        1. Brain—Wounds and injuries—Juvenile literature.
        2. Brain—Diseases—Juvenile literature. 3. Neurology—Juvenile literature. I. Title.
        RD594.G64 2014
        617.4'81044—dc23   2013001346

Manufactured in the United States of America
1 – DP – 12/31/13

CONTENTS

CHAPTER 1

BRAINS
IN THE NEWS

Former Major League Soccer (MLS) star Taylor Twellman is donating his brain to science. Hopefully, he won't be giving it up anytime soon. But Twellman and scientists hope that the study of brains like his will provide valuable information about the effects of concussions and other brain injuries. Twellman, considered one of the best MLS players ever, suffered seven concussions between 2002 and 2010. A concussion occurs when the head suddenly stops moving and the brain smashes into the inside of the skull. For example, this can occur when a soccer ball hits a head or when a head hits the windshield during an auto accident. Problems related to concussions, including memory loss, headaches, and nausea, forced Twellman to announce his retirement from the New England Revolution soccer club in 2010.

Twellman tried to deal with headaches caused by his concussions for two years. "I've done everything from acupuncture to sitting in a dark room," he said at his farewell press conference.

"I'm sick and I'm injured. When you're told if you want to live your life and be healthy, then soccer needs to stop. The decision is made for you," Twellman said. "The hardest thing about this injury is that I can do zero about it." The soccer legend plans to make the best of the situation. "I hate the fact that my career has ended on a brain injury. But now I have an opportunity to educate parents and kids about concussions."

New England Revolution player Taylor Twellman warms up before a game against the Houston Dynamo in 2009. Twellman suffered several debilitating concussions during his pro soccer career.

CELEBRATE YOUR BRAIN

Our brains are what make each of us unique. Brains hold our mind and our personality. Brains are why we can remember the past and plan for our future. They let us walk and talk. They permit us to see a sunset and feel the rain. Our brains allow us to sing a song, make a new friend, and fall in love. They let us read books like this one too.

I **DANCE** to my FAVORITE music

I **FEEL** the warm SUN on my FACE

I have my own UNIQUE **IDENTITY**

I **LAUGH**, cry, SMILE, get upset, excited, HAPPY

I **TALK** with my FRIENDS

I can **SOLVE** complicated PROBLEMS

I **UNDERSTAND** REASON and logic

I **LISTEN** to a BIRD'S SONG

I **SEE** my SURROUNDINGS

I **KNOW** the NAMES of all the PLANETS

I **PLAY** BASEBALL I HIT, run, CATCH pitch, STEAL BASE

WHAT IS TRAUMATIC BRAIN INJURY?

Traumatic brain injury (TBI) is one of the leading causes of death and disability worldwide. *Traumatic brain injury* is the term for injuries to the brain caused by blows to the head or by objects such as bullets penetrating the skull. TBI injuries range from concussion (a mild brain injury) to coma (a state of prolonged unconsciousness due to severe brain injury). TBIs may result in temporary or permanent changes in the normal function of the brain. They may also result in death.

Even though concussions are the mildest form of brain injury, they can be very serious. Concussion symptoms fall into four categories: problems with thinking and memory, physical signs, changes to emotion and mood, and problems with sleep.

Anyone who is hit in the head could have a concussion and should be evaluated by a medical professional. Danger signs that a person needs immediate medical attention include these:

- *a headache that gets worse and doesn't go away*
- *weakness, numbness, or decreased coordination in any part of the body*
- *repeated vomiting or nausea*
- *slurred speech or words that don't make sense*
- *very drowsy or cannot be awakened*
- *one pupil in the eye is larger than the other*
- *seizures*
- *trouble recognizing people or places*
- *confused, restless, or agitated*
- *a loss of consciousness, even for a short time*

TBI CAN HAPPEN TO ANYONE

People of all ages experience brain injuries. An angry parent shakes a baby, causing the brain to slosh around in the skull. Shaken baby syndrome may result in severe brain damage or death. An eight-year-old falls off his bike and hits his head. A fifteen-year-old soccer player injures herself doing a header (using the head to play, pass, or shoot the ball). Two pro football players bash helmets, and one player falls unconscious to the field. A young adult crashes her car into a tree. An improvised explosive device (IED) injures a soldier in Afghanistan. A grandfather falls from a ladder. TBIs happen most often among children from birth to four years old, adolescents aged fifteen to nineteen, and adults sixty-five years and older.

It is difficult to know exactly how many TBIs occur each year because so many people with concussions never seek medical care. They may not realize they have a concussion or may not

THINKING/ REMEMBERING

- Difficulty thinking clearly
- Feeling slowed down
- Difficulty concentrating
- Difficulty remembering new information

EMOTIONAL/ MOOD

- Irritability
- Sadness
- More emotional
- Nervousness or anxiety

PHYSICAL

- Headache
- Nausea or vomiting (early on)
- Balance problems
- Dizziness
- Fuzzy or blurry vision
- Feeling tired, having no energy
- Sensitivity to noise or light

SLEEP DISTURBANCE

- Sleeping more than usual
- Sleeping less than usual
- Trouble falling asleep

SYMPTOMS OF A CONCUSSION

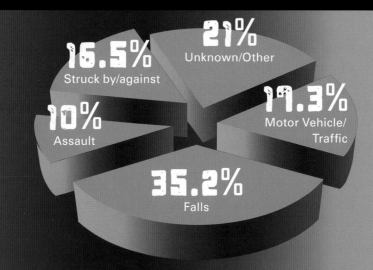

21% Unknown/Other

16.5% Struck by/against

10% Assault

19.3% Motor Vehicle/ Traffic

35.2% Falls

CAUSES OF TBI (IN THE UNITED STATES)

understand how serious a concussion can be. The US Centers for Disease Control and Prevention (CDC) is the agency that tracks and reports on national and global health issues. The CDC says hospital records show 1.7 million Americans are diagnosed with a TBI each year. Of those people, about 52,000 die of their injuries. Another 275,000 are admitted for further hospital care, while the rest are treated and released from the emergency room (ER).

Another 1.6 to 3.8 million people may experience concussions that are not officially diagnosed because they don't go to a hospital or see a doctor. In total, as many as 5.5 million TBIs ranging from mild to severe may occur each year in the United States. That's enough people to fill the Rose Bowl Stadium in Pasadena, California, sixty-one times over!

TBI IN THE NEWS

In recent years, two types of TBIs have become big news. First, sports-related concussions are being recognized as a serious problem among athletes of all ages. Secondly, shrapnel and bombs are causing large numbers of brain injuries among American soldiers in Afghanistan and Iraq.

In the past, athletes often ignored concussions because most people don't lose consciousness when they suffer a concussion. But concussions are brain injuries, and any brain injury must be taken seriously. The sporting activities that most often send children and teens to the emergency room are bicycling, football, playground accidents, and basketball. Among college athletes, football, women's ice hockey, and men's ice hockey cause the largest number of concussions. Football, ice hockey, and soccer are the sports that produce the most concussions among professional athletes. Sports-related concussions and head injuries can occur when players collide, head a soccer ball, or fall to the ice or playing field. They can occur when athletes are hit with objects such as balls or bats.

So many American soldiers have suffered TBIs that military doctors call it the signature injury of the Iraq and Afghanistan wars. The US Department of Defense (DOD) reports 266,810 members of the military sustained a TBI between 2000 and 2012. The DOD only counts the TBIs that have been diagnosed by a doctor. It's likely that thousands more soldiers have suffered TBIs and have not yet been diagnosed.

VISIT TO A BRAIN BANK

So where is Taylor Twellman's brain going when he's done with it? He's one of more than five hundred athletes who will donate their brains to Boston University's Center for the Study of Traumatic Encephalopathy (CSTE) when they die. Chronic traumatic encephalopathy (CTE) is a brain disease that causes brain tissue to die. It's found in athletes such as boxers and in other people with a history of repeated brain trauma. Examples include football players who receive numerous concussions from tough tackles and hard hits. The disease has also been found in people whose head injuries were so mild they had few or no symptoms.

Boston University has a program to study the effects of multiple concussions on the human brain. In December 2012, the center released the results of a major study of brain tissue from eighty-five people with histories of repeated head trauma before their deaths. These included football and hockey players, military veterans, and boxers.

The results astonished researchers. Sixty-eight of the brains showed the degenerative changes of CTE. These changes can begin many years or even decades after the last brain injury. Fifty of the samples were from people who had played football, ranging from a seventeen-year-old high school student to professional players from the National Football League. The brains resembled those of elderly people with degenerative diseases of the brain and nervous system.

Further studies are under way to develop ways to diagnose CTE in living people. This would allow for detection and treatment at an early stage.

Athletes, coaches, parents, and doctors are learning about the dangers of even seemingly mild brain injuries. Some brain injuries, such as those sustained in war and auto accidents, are difficult to avoid. However, many TBIs can be prevented or their effects greatly lessened by sticking to sports guidelines, using proper equipment, and following medical advice when a concussion occurs. The CDC says: "It's better to miss one game than the whole season."

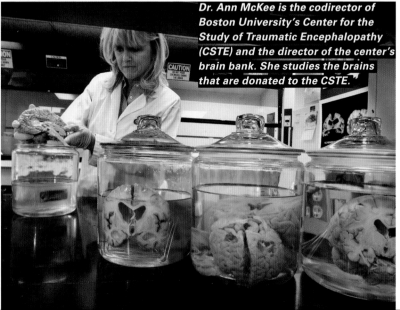

Dr. Ann McKee is the codirector of Boston University's Center for the Study of Traumatic Encephalopathy (CSTE) and the director of the center's brain bank. She studies the brains that are donated to the CSTE.

DOCTORS LOOK AT BOOGAARD'S BRAIN

National Hockey League (NHL) player Derek Boogaard died in 2011 at the age of twenty-eight of an accidental drug and alcohol overdose. His family agreed to donate his brain to the Boston University brain bank. After examining Boogaard's brain, Dr. Ann McKee diagnosed the early stages of chronic traumatic encephalopathy.

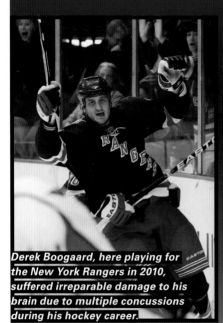

Derek Boogaard, here playing for the New York Rangers in 2010, suffered irreparable damage to his brain due to multiple concussions during his hockey career.

Such brain damage can be associated with memory loss, confusion, poor impulse control, aggression, and depression. A person with this type of damage can also develop dementia, the gradual loss of intellectual functions. Scientists predicted Boogaard would have developed dementia by middle age if he had lived.

Boogaard was recovering from a concussion when he died. He had been diagnosed with post-concussion syndrome twice. His family said he "saw stars" after being hit in the head two weeks before his final game. Boogaard spoke of having his "bell rung" (a term athletes use for a mild concussion) at least twenty times. Boogaard was considered by many to be the toughest fighter in the NHL. In May 2013, Boogaard's family filed a wrongful death suit against the NHL, saying that he died because of brain damage and drug abuse caused by the multiple head injuries he had suffered during his time with the NHL.

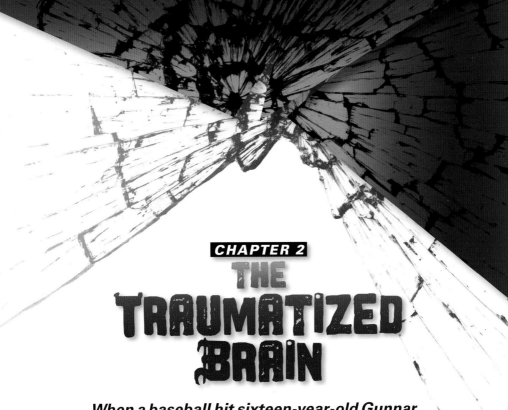

CHAPTER 2
THE TRAUMATIZED BRAIN

When a baseball hit sixteen-year-old Gunnar Sandberg of Northern California in the head during baseball practice, he collapsed in a heap on the pitcher's mound. He got up and tried to shake it off. Gunnar's dad suspected it was a concussion and anticipated that Gunnar would go to the hospital for observation only. But Gunnar's injury was much more serious than a concussion. The ball, traveling an estimated 100 miles (161 kilometers) an hour fractured Gunnar's skull.

Gunnar suffered a severe traumatic brain injury. Surgeons in the hospital removed part of his skull to allow room for his brain to swell without further damage. Using medication, the doctors also put Gunnar into a medically induced coma so his brain could rest. (A medically induced coma keeps patients unconscious and gives the brain time to heal in such a way that the person does not experience pain or anxiety.) When doctors stopped the medication a few days later, Gunnar didn't wake up. Doctors told his parents that he might not survive. But Gunnar did wake up—three weeks later.

Gunnar spent another month in rehabilitation, where he learned to walk, talk, and feed himself again. While experts said Gunnar had a remarkable recovery, he struggles with short-term memory loss and language comprehension. "School is a lot harder for me," Gunnar says. "I go to class and try to listen to everything, but my attention is a little shorter now and there's definitely some memory loss. I try to write down things a couple times and teach it to myself."

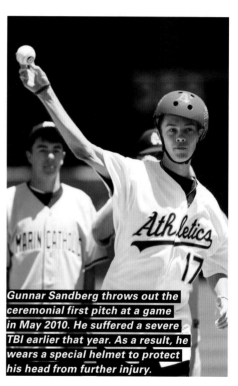

Gunnar Sandberg throws out the ceremonial first pitch at a game in May 2010. He suffered a severe TBI earlier that year. As a result, he wears a special helmet to protect his head from further injury.

MEET YOUR BRAIN

Weighing in at a mere 3 pounds (1.4 kilograms), the human brain is far more complex than any computer that scientists could ever build. The brain holds one billion nerve cells—about the same as the number of stars in our galaxy. These nerve cells are called neurons. They transmit and process information between parts of the brain. A neuron is like a tiny tree. At one end is the cell body surrounded by branches called dendrites. Dendrites receive input from other neurons. The axon is like a trunk that carries electrical impulses from one neuron to the next. The axons almost—but not quite—touch other neurons. The roots, or tips, of the axons transmit electrical and chemical signals across the space from the axon to the dendrites of the next neuron.

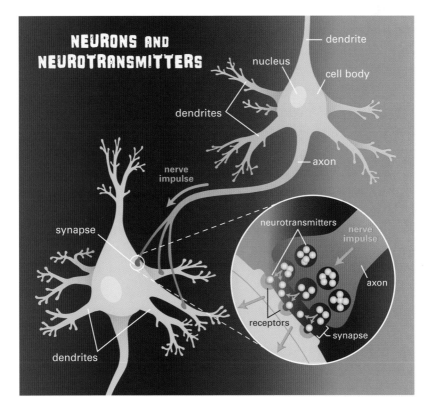

The brain is a hungry organ. It makes up only 2 percent of a person's total body weight. Yet the brain gobbles up one-fourth of the body's energy-producing glucose. And the brain uses one-fifth of the body's oxygen. The energy used by the brain is enough to light up a 25-watt lightbulb—or to ignite a million megawatt idea.

This incredibly powerful organ is one of the most delicate parts of the body. The brain is three-fourths water with a little fat, protein, and carbohydrate thrown in. The brain's texture is similar to gelatin or custard.

Our most important organ comes with its very own protective system. The hard bones of the skull are the first line of defense. And between the skull and the brain itself are three layers of membranes called meninges. The meninges are separated by a clear liquid called cerebrospinal fluid, which cushions the brain. Yet even with these built-in safeguards, the brain is easily injured.

CLOSED HEAD INJURIES

A traumatic brain injury can occur when an object such as a baseball hits the head or when the head hits an object such as a windshield. The impact causes several things to happen. First, the brain is injured at the point of impact. Second, the brain bounces inside the skull and can be injured opposite the point of impact. Third, the brain may twist as it rebounds inside the skull, damaging huge numbers of axons.

Damaged axons can no longer effectively transmit messages from one neuron to the next. Instead, only parts of the messages reach their intended target. This can leave a person feeling dazed and confused and unable to think clearly.

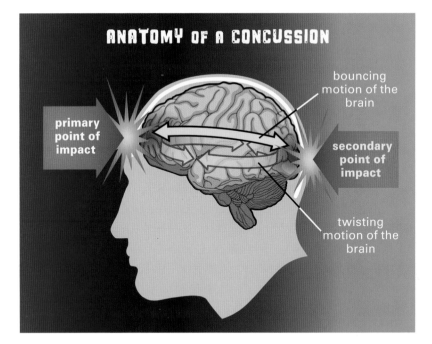

ANATOMY OF A CONCUSSION

primary point of impact

secondary point of impact

bouncing motion of the brain

twisting motion of the brain

Closed head injuries can be classified as mild, moderate, or severe. Symptoms and brain imaging results associated with each classification are the following:

CONCUSSION/MILD TBI: a confused or disoriented state lasting less than twenty-four hours; loss of consciousness for up to thirty minutes; memory loss lasting less than twenty-four hours. Brain imaging (MRI or CT scan) shows normal results.

MODERATE TBI: a confused or disoriented state lasting more than twenty-four hours; loss of consciousness between thirty minutes and twenty-four hours; memory loss between one and seven days. Brain imaging may be normal or abnormal.

SEVERE TBI: a confused or disoriented state lasting more than twenty-four hours; loss of consciousness for more than twenty-four hours; memory loss for more than seven days. Brain imaging may be normal or abnormal.

A lot can go wrong when someone suffers a closed head injury. The injured brain swells, much like a thumb swells when hit by a hammer. Unlike a thumb, however, the brain is enclosed in a tightly fitting skull. In some cases, doctors must remove a section of the skull to make room for the brain to swell safely without causing further damage. A hard impact can cause bleeding inside the brain or a blood clot may form. Depending on the location and size of the clot or bleeding, surgeons may need to cut through the skull and into the brain to stop the bleeding or remove the clot. About three out of four TBIs are mild concussions and people recover quickly without surgery.

Whether mild, moderate, or severe, concussions can be dangerous. The force of an impact can be enormous. In a Purdue University study, researchers placed sensors that measure impact inside the helmets of high school football players. Some of the helmet-to-helmet hits reached 100 Gs or more. That's one hundred times the force of gravity! By comparison, heading a soccer ball produces around 20 Gs. Brains cannot tolerate these forces without injury.

CONCUSSIONS

What actually happens to a brain during a concussion? Most people with concussions do not lose consciousness. And most concussed brains appear normal on imaging scans such as CTs or MRIs. Instead, damage occurs at the cellular level. The blow to the head injures neurons in a wide area. If the brain twists during impact, large numbers of axons that connect neurons are injured as well. Normal blood flow is interrupted. Abnormally large amounts of calcium collect in neurons. Damaged cells swell. These injuries lead to cell death. The normal electrical functioning of the brain is disrupted, much like a malfunctioning motherboard in a computer. The brain keeps on going but performs poorly.

People with concussions, even mild ones, can experience symptoms such as headaches, dizziness, nausea, and vomiting. They may have problems with balance and concentration. They can feel dazed, foggy, and unable to remember recent events. Hypersensitivity to light and noise is common. The symptoms gradually improve in days or a few weeks. In most cases, people recover completely.

CONCUSSION COMPLICATIONS

It takes some people longer than others to return to normal after a concussion. *Post-concussion syndrome* is the term used for persistent, long-lasting concussion symptoms. Experts at the Mayo Clinic say most concussion symptoms disappear within three months. However, with post-concussion syndrome, symptoms may last a year or more. The risk of developing post-concussion syndrome appears to be unrelated to the severity of the injury.

Symptoms of post-concussion syndrome are much the same as those of concussion. They include headache, dizziness, insomnia, poor memory and concentration, and mental symptoms such as depression, irritability, and anxiety. These symptoms can affect daily life. They make it difficult to perform well at school and at work.

Having multiple concussions is also a cause for concern. For example, students with two or more concussions have shown lower grade point averages than students who have not had any concussions. And people who have had three or more concussions are at higher risk of losing consciousness with a subsequent concussion. They are also more likely to have longer-lasting problems with memory and confusion than is someone who has had only one concussion.

Second impact syndrome is the term for a rare but potentially fatal condition. It occurs when a person suffers a second concussion before fully recovering from the first. It may happen hours, days, or weeks after the first event. The second impact may cause severe brain swelling, which shuts down blood circulation to large areas of the brain. Death may occur within minutes. All known cases of second-impact syndrome have occurred in children and teens.

Nathan Stiles of Spring Hill, Kansas, was seventeen years old when he died in 2010 from second impact syndrome. He was a star running back for his high school football team, a top student, and a homecoming king. Nathan suffered a concussion in a game in early October. Doctors kept Nathan off the field for nearly three weeks, clearing him to return to play on October 22. He had several hard hits during that game but insisted he was fine. His final game was on October 28. He collapsed after complaining of severe pain in his head. Despite intensive treatment, he died the next morning from his injury. An autopsy showed that Nathan died of a blood clot in his brain related to second impact syndrome.

Chris Nowinski is with the Boston University Center for the Study of Traumatic Encephalopathy. He phoned Nathan's father the day after Nathan died to ask the family to donate

Nathan's brain. The family agreed to do so. "I've called hundreds of families within forty-eight hours of their loved ones dying and it's never easy," Nowinski said. In his conversations with families, he focuses on the fact that the brain bank's work will help other families in the future.

Dr. Ann McKee, the brain bank's director, is the doctor who looked at Nathan's brain. In January 2012, she told a reporter that Nathan's brain showed clear evidence of abnormal tau protein, commonly found in the brains of patients with Alzheimer's. Nathan is the youngest person known to have chronic traumatic encephalopathy. "You expect a pristine brain," she said. "I saw...that [Nathan's brain] was riddled with tau proteins. I was stunned at how similar that brain was to boxers who lived into their 70s."

PENETRATING HEAD INJURIES

Closed head injuries produce symptoms ranging from mild concussions to comas. However, penetrating head injuries are likely to be serious. Penetrating injuries are caused by fast-moving objects such as bullets or shrapnel that pierce the skull and enter the brain. Slower-moving objects such as knives or bone fragments from skull fractures also produce penetrating head injuries. Improvised explosive devices, or IEDs, are a major cause of penetrating head injuries among military service members.

In cases of penetrating head injuries, brain imaging results are always abnormal and show the object (bullet, shrapnel, etc.). In most cases, the foreign body will have fractured the skull on entry. The object may cause serious bleeding into the brain. Large portions of the brain may be permanently damaged. Bullets are especially dangerous because they cause extensive injury as they plow through delicate brain tissue. The area of damage can be many times the diameter of the bullet itself. Infection is also a serious problem with any penetrating head injury because a bullet or a blade is teeming with bacteria.

The incidence of penetrating injuries to the brain has dramatically increased over the past twenty years. Gunshot wounds to the head have become the leading or second-leading cause of head injury in many US cities. People who survive penetrating brain injuries are likely to be left with personality changes or problems with vision, memory, thinking, or moving. Each brain injury is different, depending on which part of the brain the penetrating object injured. And even with the best medical care, half of patients who survive a penetrating brain injury develop permanent seizures.

BY THE NUMBERS

The victim of a gunshot wound to the head is thirty-five times more likely to die than a patient with a comparable closed head injury.

Gunshot wounds cause more than one-third of TBI deaths.

One study found nine out of ten people with gunshot wounds to their heads died of their injuries.

THE HOLE IN PHINEAS GAGE'S HEAD

Phineas Gage was the foreman on a railroad construction crew in 1848. While the crew was blasting rocks in preparation to lay railroad track in Vermont, an explosion sent a pointed iron rod through his skull and brain. The rod flew 80 feet (24 meters) after leaving Gage's skull. The doctor who took care of Gage saw his brain pulsating through the hole. Against all odds, Gage lived for nearly twelve years after the accident. He died of seizures caused by his injury.

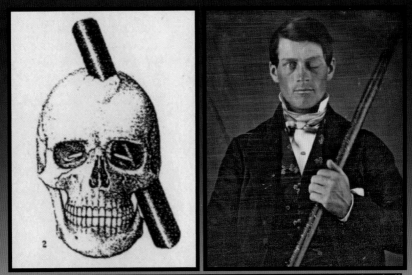

This illustration from 1850 (left) shows where an iron rod lodged in the skull of Phineas Gage, penetrating his brain after an accident during railroad construction in 1848. Gage (shown right, holding the iron rod) survived the accident, but related personality changes impacted him for the rest of his life.

CHAPTER 3

SPORTS-RELATED CONCUSSIONS

Meet fifteen-year-old Allison Kasacavage of Pennsylvania. She's recovering from a series of concussions she suffered while playing soccer. Her first concussion happened when she ran into another player on the field. "When I got up, my head was pounding," Allison said. "There was a heartbeat in my head and I had no idea what it was. I was just so confused." She returned to play but was nervous about heading the ball. "If you don't head the ball, you're the weakest link." Allison's parents knew about the danger of concussions in football. They didn't realize soccer players also got concussions until it happened to Allison.

Allison had received five concussions as of

2012. Three of them happened while playing soccer. Two others occurred when she fell at home as a result of concussion-related dizziness. Allison no longer plays soccer. Because of headaches, dizziness, and inability to focus for long periods of time, she is able to attend school only four hours a day. She uses a blue light in her bedroom to ease her headaches. "It's almost like I need a sign on my back saying, 'My head is broken.' You can't see [a concussion]. It's not visible. Not many people understand."

Dr. Robert Cantu is a neurosurgeon and an expert in concussions. He says, "People who think of concussions as being present mostly in guys and mostly in the sport of football are just plain wrong. Soccer is right at the top of the list for girls." Girls make up nearly half the three million players in US Youth Soccer leagues. "Many of these individuals are going to go on to post-concussion syndrome, which can alter their ability to function at a high level for the rest of their lives," Cantu says. He believes heading should be outlawed in soccer for players under fourteen years old.

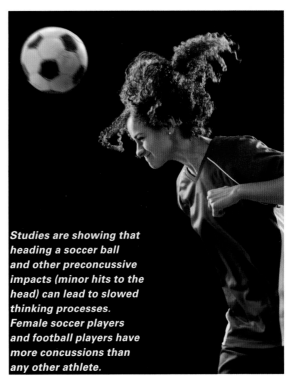

Studies are showing that heading a soccer ball and other preconcussive impacts (minor hits to the head) can lead to slowed thinking processes. Female soccer players and football players have more concussions than any other athlete.

SCHOOL SPORTS AND CONCUSSIONS

For decades athletes considered "getting your bell rung" to be a normal part of sports. Athletes played down concussion symptoms so they could return to the game as soon as possible. In recent years, researchers are ringing bells of their own—alarm bells—about the growing evidence that even minor concussions can cause permanent brain damage.

Playing sports in school can be a lot of fun. It can also be dangerous if you get hit in the head. One recent study identified more than half a million visits to US emergency rooms for concussions during a four-year period among patients eight to nineteen years old. That's about the same number of people as the entire population of Tucson, Arizona. Half the concussions were related to sporting activities.

Concussions in children and teens are on the rise. Experts say this is because more concussions are likely being identified than in previous years and more kids are playing sports. In one four-year period, for example, sports-related concussions doubled in middle school students and more than doubled among high school students. And that's just for concussions treated in the hospital. Thousands of concussions are treated in doctors' offices or aren't reported at all.

Concussions can occur in any sport. Among eight- to thirteen-year-old athletes, concussions occur most often in football, basketball, baseball, and soccer. In high school, the greatest number of concussions occurs in football, girls' soccer, boys' lacrosse, girls' lacrosse, and boys' soccer. Many athletes fail to report their concussions to coaches, trainers, or parents. Why don't athletes report concussions? An article in *Time* magazine gave these reasons:

- *They didn't think it was serious enough to report (66 percent).*
- *They didn't want to leave the game (41 percent).*
- *They didn't know it was a concussion (36 percent).*
- *They didn't want to let teammates down (22 percent).*

THE GENDER GAP

Concussions affect boys and girls differently. One study found headaches are the most common symptom of concussions in both genders. However, boys report being confused and having amnesia far more often after concussions than girls do. Girls report feeling more tired and being more sensitive to noise than boys. While this study did not investigate why symptoms differ by gender, a previous study suggested it may be due to the hormonal differences between boys and girls.

Boys are more likely to suffer concussions from running into other players. Girls are more likely to get them from being hit with balls or falling down. Overall, boys have about three times as many concussions as girls do. That's probably because more boys play in more sports. However, girls have a higher rate of concussion than boys when playing similar sports. Concussion expert Dr. Cantu says, "Studies show girls report nearly twice as many concussions as boys in sports they both play."

BY THE NUMBERS

High school football players report up to sixty-seven thousand concussions per year.

Half of concussed football players don't report their concussions.

At least 5 percent of all high school athletes suffer concussions each year.

LET'S HEAR FROM THE CHEERLEADERS

- About 3.6 million cheerleaders root for their teams each year.

- Many of the twenty-six thousand injuries each year among cheerleaders are head and neck injuries.

- Cheerleading injuries are the most common cause of catastrophic brain and spinal injuries among female high school athletes.

Cheerleaders perform acrobatic routines without safety features such as nets. A fall on the head during a routine can lead to devastating head injuries. Because many schools do not recognize cheerleading as a sport, safety regulations are not mandatory.

Girls are more likely to be concussed than boys for several reasons. First, girls may report injuries more often. Secondly, girls have weaker neck muscles and a smaller head mass than boys. This makes it more likely a girl would sustain a concussion than would a boy with similar injuries. In addition, some sports, such as ice hockey, allow body checking (driving the top half of the body into an opponent) on boys' teams but not on girls' teams. Girls may therefore be less prepared to protect themselves from a head injury when an accidental collision occurs.

A REFEREE SPEAKS OUT

Dr. Lori McGowan is a lacrosse referee in Pennsylvania. She describes the symptoms of concussion that people should look for if children or young people are injured while playing sports: "Changes in mood, sleeping patterns, activity levels, appetite and behavior can point to a possible concussion." Dr. McGowan sees how concussions affect young athletes. After watching a middle school girls' lacrosse game, she noted, "During the first eight minutes of the game there were three injuries, one related to a child's head." She went on to explain, "The player was checked from behind. She fell and hit her head on the turf and began seizing. To my dismay, she returned to play in less than three weeks. She went on to have another concussion

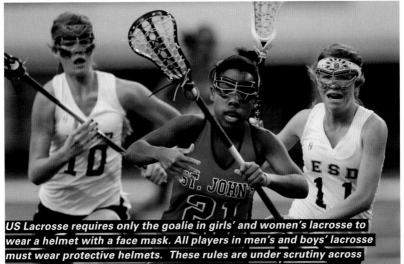

US Lacrosse requires only the goalie in girls' and women's lacrosse to wear a helmet with a face mask. All players in men's and boys' lacrosse must wear protective helmets. These rules are under scrutiny across the country as more females participate in sports and sustain TBIs.

and seizure. She is now barred from impact sports for the rest of her life."

While male lacrosse players must wear protective helmets, they're optional for females. Dr. McGowan wants to see this changed. "All female lacrosse players should wear helmets because it's a competitive contact sport."

COLLEGE ATHLETES

People may think football is the most hazardous college sport. However, a study of National Collegiate Athletic Association (NCAA) athletes found more concussions occur in women's ice hockey than in any other college sport. Football and men's ice hockey have the next highest concussion rates.

About one-third of college football players report having had one concussion, while one-fifth report having had two or more. Concussions can impair information processing, problem solving, planning, and memory. That's bad news for anyone. However, for a college student, these problems can mean the difference between completing a degree and dropping out of school.

In 2010 the NCAA put new guidelines for college team sports into place. Each school is required to have a concussion management plan. The plan requires the following:

- *Athletes are informed of concussion symptoms at the start of each season.*
- *Athletes sign a statement agreeing to report concussion symptoms to medical staff.*
- *Athletes who have a concussion must be removed from the sport for at least one day.*

- *Athletes cannot return to play until a team doctor clears them to participate after symptoms are gone.*

Are the new guidelines helping to reduce concussions? It's hard to say. A study of football players from the US Naval, Military, and Air Force Academies found that concussions nearly doubled during the 2010–2011 season. According to Dr. Kelly Kilcoyne, one of the study's authors, "The timing of the new NCAA regulations and the increase in reported concussions could be attributed to underreporting in the past. But such an increase is still notable. We need continued studies in football and other sports to find out more."

Dr. Robert Glatter is an emergency room physician in a New York hospital. He treats concussions and says that young adults are especially vulnerable to brain injury. "Their brains continue to develop into their early 20s, and research has shown that younger athletes, all other factors being equal, will typically require more time to recover from concussions than their adult counterparts. If they sustain head trauma or concussions in their late teens and early 20s, the long-term complications . . . can have lasting effects on younger athletes into their adult years."

THE PROS

Watching professional football games has long been a favorite pastime in the United States. Americans love the fierce team rivalries, the Hail Mary pass, and the *thunk* of helmets smashing together. The prevalence of sports-related concussions seems to be highest among professional athletes in the National Football League (NFL). One study found at least six out of ten NFL players had suffered at least one concussion while one-fourth of the players admitted to three or more. Concussed players report headaches and problems with memory, concentration, and speech.

Another recent study looked at six hundred retired NFL players who had suffered three or more concussions. Those players were three times more likely to be depressed than players who had not had concussions. And a study published in 2011 found former football players have more cognitive difficulties (problems related to perception, memory, judgment, and reasoning) in later life than other former athletes and nonathletes.

Head injuries are common in football. In fact, estimates suggest that up to 40 percent of football players experience a concussion each year. Most of them go unreported.

WHEN GOOD BRAINS GO BAD

Junior Seau, twelve-time NFL All-Pro linebacker, retired in 2009 after twenty years of playing football for San Diego, Miami, and New England. His family said he had experienced wild mood swings, forgetfulness, insomnia, and depression since retirement. He hid his symptoms well in public, but not from family or friends. "He emotionally detached himself and would kind of go away," son Tyler Seau said. "And then the depression. . . . It started to get progressively worse."

In May 2012, Seau committed suicide by shooting himself in the chest. After Seau's death, his family asked scientists to examine his brain tissue. Study results, released in January 2013, showed Seau had CTE, which is linked to repeated head trauma such as football players experience when sustaining concussions.

Scientists have found similar damage in the brains of other former football players who killed themselves. These players include Dave Duerson, defensive back for the Chicago Bears; Andre Waters, defensive back for the Philadelphia Eagles; and Ray Easterling, safety for the Atlantic Falcons. They join a list of several dozen college and professional football players whose brains showed CTE at their deaths.

Studies linking NFL players to permanent brain damage are ongoing. An especially chilling study was published in 2012. It found NFL players were more likely to die of diseases that damage brain cells than are average Americans. Specifically, the risk of death from Alzheimer's disease and amyotrophic lateral sclerosis (ALS), or Lou Gehrig's disease, was four times greater among NFL players than among other professional athletes. Both diseases are progressive degenerative disorders of the nervous system. Alzheimer's affects nerve cells in the brain. It causes loss of memory, thinking, and language skills as well as problematic behavioral changes. ALS affects nerve cells in the brain and the spinal cord that are responsible for movement. As cells die, the brain can no longer control muscle movement. ALS patients have problems swallowing and breathing. They can become totally paralyzed. Both diseases are fatal.

Professional ice hockey also has a long history of concussions. It's not unusual for National Hockey League players to miss dozens of games each season because of concussions. For example, Sidney Crosby of the Pittsburgh Penguins missed the final forty-one games of the 2010–2011 season and the first twenty games of the 2011–2012 season due to concussions.

Professional hockey players may receive as many as three hundred head hits each year. Brian Rolston, a forward with the New York Islanders hockey team, had his "bell rung" in 2011. He didn't know he had a concussion until he realized he couldn't answer simple questions. When doctors evaluated Rolston, he had difficulty reciting the months of the year in reverse order.

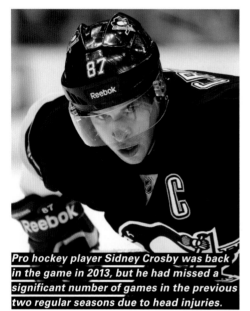
Pro hockey player Sidney Crosby was back in the game in 2013, but he had missed a significant number of games in the previous two regular seasons due to head injuries.

"Then I couldn't name the last team I played against," he said. "I failed the test." Within two days, Rolston was experiencing headaches and dizziness.

NHL deputy commissioner Bill Daly says the concussion issue is difficult. "The NHL is working to raise the level of awareness on the issue among our clubs, coaching and training staffs, team physicians, and players," he said in an interview with USA Today. "The focus and attention this issue is receiving is a direct result of our collective efforts to raise awareness of the seriousness of the issue."

Can sports-related concussions be prevented or at least decreased? Professional sports organizations along with their college and high school counterparts are looking at ways to do just that. For example, in 2011 the NFL changed the kickoff rule. The rule moved kickoff from the thirty-yard line to the thirty-five yard line. The NFL reported a 40 percent drop in concussions on that play because players catching the ball are less likely to be forcefully tackled when they are farther from the touchdown zone.

CHANGING THE CULTURE OF SPORTS

Some experts believe sports culture itself needs to change. An article in Time magazine in 2010 about professional football recommended the following:

> **CHANGE THE RULES. Take the purposeful helmet hit out of football. Institute a penalty for egregious head hits.**
> **CHANGE THE EQUIPMENT AND TRAINING. Continue to develop better helmets. Consider eliminating some off-season training that unnecessarily results in head injuries.**

CHANGE YOUTH FOOTBALL. *Train all youth coaches in concussion-management programs. Coaches should use a concussion assessment card. They should rethink techniques taught to children.*

CHANGE THE CULTURE. *Teach players about the dangers of concussion and encourage them to report it. Many young athletes are victims of their own bravado.*

Better helmets are helping to reduce concussions. Kevin Guskiewicz is a professor at the University of North Carolina and an expert on football helmets. "With improved soft materials inside the hard outer shell, a modern helmet can lessen the effect of an impact," he said. "Athletes in football, hockey and lacrosse can receive more than 160 times the force of gravity when tackled or checked."

CHAPTER 4
ASSESSING AND TREATING CONCUSSIONS

Quarterback Brady Quinn of the Kansas City Chiefs remembers October 28, 2012, very well. He took a knee to the back of his head during a game with the Oakland Raiders. But he wasn't about to let that stop him from playing. He'd waited three years to be the starting quarterback. A concussion wasn't going to sideline him. "I tried to stay in the game because it was the first opportunity for me in a while," Quinn said after his injury. "I tried to play through it and that's my fault for not being smart about it."

Quinn later admitted to experiencing tunnel vision after the impact. He was so dazed he put on the wrong helmet to go back onto the field. When he threw an interception, he couldn't even see the Oakland player he aimed for. That's when coaches pulled Quinn from the game. This was Quinn's second concussion. He'd been hit so hard during a preseason game at Green Bay a few weeks earlier that he blacked out for a few seconds and saw stars. He stayed in that game as well because his vision quickly improved.

Quinn knows about the risk of repeated concussions and that they've been linked to dementia among former players. That risk remains in the back of his mind. "It's definitely a thought," he says, "because it's the second one this year, and if you come back too soon, before your symptoms calm down, it does involve some risk."

Doctors cleared Quinn for light exercise a few weeks later. However, they weren't certain when he could return to full play.

Kansas City Chiefs quarterback Brady Quinn warmed up before a game in October 2012 from which he was eventually pulled after a serious head injury. Athletes often hide the effects of head injury in order to keep playing.

ASSESSING CONCUSSIONS

Once Brady Quinn reported his concussion, his team did everything right. They pulled him from the game immediately and evaluated him. Anyone who sustains a head injury should be evaluated by a health-care professional or by a person trained to assess concussions. At high school games, trainers and coaches can learn how to do concussion assessments. If nurses or paramedics are present, they can assess too. At pro games, doctors and ambulances staffed with paramedics wait nearby to take injured players to an emergency room if necessary for in-depth evaluation.

Injured players can be screened quickly on the sidelines for a concussion. One test is called the SCAT2 (Sports Concussion Assessment Tool 2). The injured player answers a list of questions. Does he have a headache or dizziness? Vision problems? Feeling dazed or confused? The examiner will ask if the athlete knows where the team is playing, what the score is, and

A high school trainer administers a simple vision test called the Confrontation Visual Field Test, or CVFT. Standing at arm's length from the player, she asks him if he can see her fingers in different areas of his field of vision. Problems with vision occur among about 20 to 40 percent of all people with TBI.

what inning or quarter it is. Because most concussions don't cause loss of consciousness, it's important to ask about other symptoms the injured athlete may be experiencing, such as memory or balance problems.

Other assessment tools include concussion-testing apps downloadable on smartphones. This makes it even easier for the examiner to tell if a player has received a concussion. Depending on test results, a player may be benched for the rest of the game, sent home, or taken to an emergency room.

Some high school, college, and pro sports organizations are performing preseason screening of athletes' neurological, psychological, and cognitive functions. If a concussion occurs, results can be measured against baseline testing. These tests are computerized and more complex than sideline tests. They

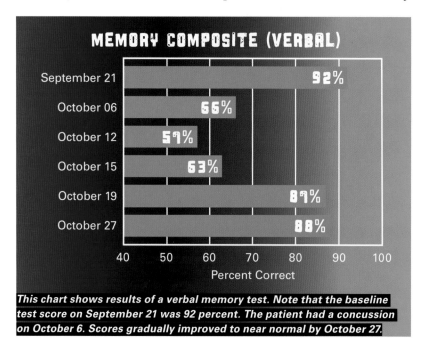

MEMORY COMPOSITE (VERBAL)

September 21	92%
October 06	66%
October 12	57%
October 15	63%
October 19	87%
October 27	88%

Percent Correct

This chart shows results of a verbal memory test. Note that the baseline test score on September 21 was 92 percent. The patient had a concussion on October 6. Scores gradually improved to near normal by October 27.

may be given several times during recovery from a concussion to monitor the injured athlete's progress. One test widely used for this purpose is called imPACT (Immediate Post-Concussion Assessment and Cognitive Testing). The twenty-minute test includes a description of current symptoms and injury. It measures word and visual memory; cognitive processing speed; matching symbols, letters, and numbers; attention span; and reaction time.

A 2010 study of 550 concussions among high school athletes showed those who received tests such as ImPACT or SCAT2 were less likely to return to play within a week of their injury. Some researchers recommend that athletes should not return to play until they've been free of symptoms for at least a week. Athletes who return to play too early may have a more serious injury if they suffer another concussion.

TREATING CONCUSSIONS

Another study in 2012 looked at nearly fifteen thousand concussions in high school students. The most commonly reported symptoms were a headache, dizziness, and difficulty with concentration. People with concussions also may find it difficult to perform their daily activities, whether it's going to school or to work. How fast people recover depends on age, state of health, the severity of the injury, and how they take care of themselves after the concussion.

For concussions without complications, time is the only real treatment. People with concussions need both physical and cognitive rest. Cognitive rest means resting the brain as well as the body. It means no school, work, reading, texting, phoning, gaming, or television until a doctor says so. A brain that is actively thinking, interacting with others, or playing a computer game is not a brain at rest. As the days go by, the doctor may approve a person's return to school or work on a part-time basis.

AMERICAN ACADEMY OF NEUROLOGY 2013 SPORTS CONCUSSION GUIDELINES AND RECOMMENDATIONS

These new guidelines assist health-care providers to better assess and treat sports-related concussions. They are based on an analysis of all published evidence-based research on clinical risk factors, diagnostic tools, and interventions that may reduce further concussion risk and enhance recovery.

- Before participating in sports: Licensed health-care professionals (LHCPs) should educate school and sports staff, and athletes and families about concussion risks.

- When a concussion is suspected: LHCPs educated in sideline concussion assessment tools should administer these in conjunction with evaluation of the possibly concussed athlete. Team personnel (coaches, trainers, etc.) should immediately remove athletes with possible concussions from play. Athletes should not return to play until assessed by an LCHP trained in the diagnosis and management of traumatic brain injury.

However, many TBIs are moderate or severe. While treatment for mild traumatic brain injuries such as concussion is relatively simple, more serious brain injuries require intense medical care.

- **Management of a diagnosed concussion:** Athletes must not return to play or even practice (if there is risk of contact) after concussion until all symptoms have resolved and the athlete is off any medication prescribed to treat the concussion.

- **Age:** Athletes of high school age and younger with diagnosed concussion should be treated more conservatively than older athletes.

- **Return to play or retirement:** LHCPs should consider using tools to measure cognitive function to determine recovery. LHCPs should prescribe individual plans allowing gradual return to physical activity. LHCPs may recommend that athletes with a history of multiple concussions seek advanced testing and counseling. Athletes with persistent symptoms should be counseled about the risks of further concussion and the need to consider permanent retirement from contact sports.

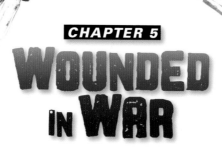

CHAPTER 5

WOUNDED in WAR

Staff Sergeant Scott Lilley was twenty-seven years old in 2007 when an explosion nearly killed him in the war in Iraq (2003–2011). He was the gunner in a Humvee returning to camp after a mission. Just 1 mile (1.6 km) from base, an enemy bomb exploded under his Humvee. A piece of shrapnel hit Lilley in the head. Lilley remained conscious for the fifteen minutes it took for his buddies to get him to the nearest combat support hospital.

Lilley was airlifted to the American hospital in Balad, Iraq. Surgeons found the BB-sized piece of shrapnel had barreled to the center of his brain. It was so deep that doctors felt it would be more dangerous to remove it than to leave it in place. Two days later, Scott was flown to Landstuhl Regional Medical Center in Germany. Doctors phoned Scott's parents in New Mexico to tell them about his injury. Although Lilley was not expected to live, he moved his fingers for the first time when he heard his mom's voice on the phone.

A medically equipped military plane carried Lilley and other wounded soldiers to Walter Reed Army Medical Center near Washington, DC. President George W. Bush was among the dignitaries meeting the plane when it landed. Lilley spent the next few months in rehabilitation hospitals, where therapists taught him to walk, talk, and eat again. Lilley will live the rest of his life with the shrapnel in his brain.

Before his injury, Lilley had planned to devote his entire career to serving in the US Air Force. After rehabilitation, he returned to limited military duty. But he struggled with short-term memory problems and took a medical retirement in 2010. Lilley went on to work as a civilian with service members and veterans at an air force base.

In 2004, during the Iraq war, shrapnel slammed through Lieutenant Colonel Timothy Maxwell's cheek and into his brain. As in Scott Lilley's case, surgeons knew that removing the shrapnel could cause more brain damage, so they left it in place. Scars are evidence of Maxwell's injury.

TBI IN THE MILITARY

More than two million American service members have been deployed to Iraq and Afghanistan since terrorists attacked the United States on September 11, 2001. According to the US Department of Defense (DOD), more than 266,810 of these men and women have received a TBI in the service of their country. This number only counts people with concussions diagnosed by a doctor. Thousands of other people may have suffered TBIs and have not yet been diagnosed. The DOD classifies TBIs among American service members as the following:

MILD CONCUSSION	*76.8 percent*
MODERATE CONCUSSION	*16.6 percent*
CANNOT CLASSIFY OR UNKNOWN	*4.0 percent*
PENETRATING HEAD INJURY,	
e.g., bullet or shrapnel enters brain	*1.6 percent*
SEVERE CONCUSSION	*1.0 percent*

Traditional concussions occur when the head suddenly stops, but the brain keeps moving and smashes into the inside of the skull. This occurs in sports-related concussions, falls, and motor vehicle accidents. However, most of the concussions that occur in the military are caused by explosive blast waves tearing through the brain. Blast waves injure brains in three ways:

PRIMARY BLAST INJURY: An explosion generates a blast wave that travels faster than the speed of sound (768 miles, or 1,236 km, per hour). A high-pressure blast wave surges through helmets, skulls, and brains.

Even though the blast wave doesn't cause bleeding, it
severely damages brain cells and nerve pathways.
SECONDARY BLAST INJURY: The explosion propels
shrapnel and debris, which may hit the soldier's head
and helmet. If the object penetrates the skull and the
brain, it's called a penetrating injury.
TERTIARY BLAST INJURY: The explosion can throw the
soldier through the air to the ground or into a nearby
wall. Once the body stops, the brain continues to move.
It hits one side of the skull and bounces against the
opposite side. The brain is injured in several places.

Doctors do not completely understand how blast injuries cause TBIs. It seems that exposure to blasts differs from other causes of concussion. For example, most people in the civilian population have a complete recovery within six months after a concussion. Yet veterans often experience symptoms for eighteen to twenty-four months. The incidence of daily headaches among US soldiers after a combat-related concussion is four to five times higher than seen in the general population after concussion.

IMPROVISED EXPLOSIVE DEVICES

In previous wars, soldiers with serious head injuries usually died. However, medical care and modern military armor have become so effective that most soldiers with serious head injuries survive. Most of these head injuries are caused by improvised explosive devices.

An IED is a homemade bomb consisting of an explosive charge, a power source (usually a battery), a triggering device, and a container. The container can be as simple as an empty 5-gallon (19-liter) can of cooking oil. Bombers may pack nails and metal fragments into the IED to increase the amount of shrapnel the explosion can hurl. As in Scott Lilley's case, this causes greater injury to soldiers. IEDs can be set to explode by remote control using a cell phone or radio signal. They can also be set off with timers, wires, or by vehicles driving over them.

An IED can be small enough for one person to carry or big enough to fill a truck. While suicide bombers carry some IEDs, many are planted along the roads that troops travel. IEDs are intended to disable and destroy military vehicles and to kill and maim soldiers. They are also a major cause of civilian deaths.

IEDs have been used in war for decades. However, they became widely known during the wars in Afghanistan (2001–present) and Iraq. IEDs were the number one killer of American troops in those countries. Nearly twice as many TBIs occurred in those wars than during the Vietnam War (1957–1975). Although the number of IEDs is up, the casualty rate is decreasing because more IEDs are being located and destroyed before they explode. Even so, IEDs cause most of the traumatic brain injuries in American soldiers.

THE DAMAGES DONE

A study published in a medical journal in 2012 reported an alarming new finding about military TBIs. Researchers looked at brains of dead soldiers who had experienced blast injuries. Their brains were compared with athletes with histories of concussions. Investigators found signs of chronic traumatic encephalopathy in the military veterans with blast injuries.

The damage resembled that of athletes who had suffered repeated concussions.

Researchers realized that a single blast from an IED can cause CTE. One blast. One concussion. Permanent brain damage. People with this type of brain damage may experience personality changes, depression, and long-term problems with memory and judgment. CTE can even lead to dementia and death. Study researchers said that one out of five American service members in Iraq and Afghanistan have been exposed to blast injuries and experienced TBI. That means as many as 460,000 of the 2.3 million Americans deployed in those regions since 2001 could potentially develop CTE in the future.

THE PURPLE HEART

The Purple Heart *(right)* is a US military decoration awarded to those who have been wounded or killed while serving their country. In the past, only serious physical wounds resulting from enemy action qualified soldiers for the Purple Heart. This excluded many concussions. However, doctors have learned that concussions can be more severe than gunshot wounds. In April 2011, the US secretary of the army approved a policy allowing soldiers to be awarded the Purple Heart for concussions and mild traumatic brain injuries. The military has since awarded hundreds of Purple Hearts to service members who sustained brain injuries while in service to their country.

Many American soldiers develop post-traumatic stress disorder (PTSD), a mental health condition that can occur after traumatic events. War, assaults, accidents, and disasters are all highly emotional events known to cause PTSD. It's not unusual for people with TBIs to also have PTSD. When one person has both conditions, treatment becomes more complicated.

The military is looking for better ways to prevent and treat TBI and PTSD in US veterans. For example, the army has established nine concussion care centers in Afghanistan. Dr. Terry Rauch of the DOD says, "TBI and post-traumatic stress disorder are two of the most devastating injuries suffered by our warfighters in Iraq and Afghanistan. Identifying better treatments for those impacted is critical."

CHAPTER 6

WE ALL FALL DOWN

Marcia Henry knows what it's like to fall down and get a concussion. She fell while skiing with friends at Copper Mountain, Colorado, years ago. At the time, few skiers wore helmets. "About halfway down the mountain, I hit an icy patch in the snow and fell. My head hit the ground and I lost consciousness for several minutes. When I regained consciousness, I got up and skied down the mountain."

Marcia wandered around at the ski lodge for a while. She didn't know who she was or what she should do. "My friends found me and took me to the on-site clinic. The procedure was to observe anyone with a head injury for an hour. If there were no seizures or other serious symptoms, you could leave. I had none of those symptoms so we left after an hour. I didn't recognize my friends. I was confused and crying."

The next morning, Marcia had the worst headache of her life. She also had memory problems. "It was primarily recent memories that were gone. Most of them came back over the next week, but I never remembered the accident itself. I was disoriented for the first few weeks and had a strange feeling of unreality." The entire event left Marcia badly traumatized. "I never skied again," she said.

While sports-related concussions receive a lot of attention, falls are the leading cause of traumatic brain injury in the United States. Falls occur more often in certain age groups. For example, falls cause half the TBIs among children under fourteen years of age. And six out of ten TBIs among people sixty-five and older are caused by falls.

FALLS IN CHILDREN

Thousands of children are treated in ERs each year after they've fallen at home, at school, or while at play. Children fall on the stairs. They fall from windows. They fall in showers and tubs. They fall from tricycles and bicycles and playground equipment. Many of the falls result in TBIs. Others result in broken bones or internal injuries.

According to the CDC, falls are the leading cause of nonfatal injuries such as concussions for children and teens up to the age of nineteen. The exact number of people who sustain a concussion due to a fall is not known because many people who fall are treated in doctors' offices, where doctors are not required to report concussions. Still, the number of reported

About 75 percent of all bicycling deaths are from head injury. Most head injuries in bicycle accidents (85 percent) can be prevented by wearing a helmet.

falls is on the rise. The CDC found a 62 percent increase in fall-related TBIs seen in children at ERs between 2002 and 2006. The CDC cannot pinpoint the reason for increased falls. It could be that more people seek treatment for head injuries than in the past.

Stair-related injuries are a very common cause of falls in children. The American Academy of Pediatrics found that nearly one million children younger than five years of age were treated in ERs for stair-related injuries in a ten-year period. Many of the injuries in babies occurred when an adult fell while carrying infants down steps. Children injured in these falls were three times more likely to be hospitalized for treatment of their injury than children whose falls did not include an adult tumbling down the stairs and landing on top of them.

Falls in bathtubs and showers are another common cause of head injuries among children. Children four years of age and younger are much more likely to fall than are older children. Younger children's balance is not well developed. Their heads are larger compared to the size of their bodies than are those of older children. This tends to throw young children off-balance so they fall more easily.

Falls from windows can also cause concussions and other serious injuries. One study found that more than five thousand children are treated in ERs each year after falling from windows. The rate of injury is highest among children younger than five years old. Falling onto a hard surface or from three stories or more is likely to result in serious injuries such as TBIs.

Playground falls send more than two hundred thousand children to ERs each year. Nearly half of those falls result in serious injuries such as concussions and broken bones. Children between five and nine years of age have the most ER visits for playground-related injuries. Falls from climbing equipment and swings cause the most injuries on public playgrounds. Swings are responsible for most injuries at home. For unknown reasons, girls tend to have more injuries at playgrounds than boys do.

BY THE NUMBERS

About 8,000 children are treated in emergency rooms daily for fall-related injuries.

Nearly 35,600 children are injured each year when they slip and fall in a tub or a shower.

Many of these injuries are TBIs.

PREVENTING FALLS IN CHILDREN

Parents, teachers, teen babysitters, and other caregivers can help protect young children from falls that can result in dangerous TBIs. Many of the safety measures are easy to implement.

STAIRS. When people carry children down stairs, they should not carry anything else. Adults should hold onto the handrail with one hand at all times. Babies should not be taken down stairs in strollers or seats. Do not push a child in a stroller onto an escalator. Use the elevator. Parents should install baby gates at the top and bottom of stairs and should keep stairs free of clutter.

TUBS AND SHOWERS. Use nonslip mats or antiskid decals in tubs and showers. Grab bars or safety bars can help protect children from falling. Adults should supervise younger children who are in the tub or the shower.

WINDOWS. Most falls from windows occur in the spring and the summer when windows are likely to be open. That means people should be especially careful during those months. Parents can install window guards and window locks. Planting grass or bushes below windows can soften the impact if a child does fall.

PLAYGROUNDS. Parents, teachers, and others in charge of playgrounds should be certain the equipment is well maintained. Surfaces under playground equipment should be soft. Wood chips and sand are safer than dirt or grass. Many playgrounds have a rubber matting or surface, often made from recycled tires.

FALLS IN OLDER ADULTS

Falls among older adults can be devastating. About one-third of people over the age of sixty-five who fall suffer moderate to severe injuries such as head trauma or hip fractures. These injuries make it difficult for older people to take care of themselves. The injuries also increase the risk of death due to complications of prolonged bed rest and of immobility, such as pneumonia and blood clots.

While more women than men fall, men are much more likely to die from a fall. The number of fall-related TBIs and deaths among older adults is going up. One study looked at ER visits over a five-year period and found that visits for TBI in older adults had increased by nearly 50 percent. This could be due to more awareness of the dangers of brain injuries. The increase in the aging population is also a factor. In addition, a person doesn't have to fall very far to sustain severe TBI warranting an ER visit. In one study, nearly one-third of older people who died of TBI had fallen fewer than 10 feet (3 m).

Many factors increase the risk of falling in older adults. These include poor vision, poor balance, dizziness, changes in blood pressure, muscle weakness, and other medical problems. Doctors may be able to help patients decrease the risks of falling related to medical conditions. For example, treating dizziness and blood pressure problems can significantly decrease the risk of falls.

People can help prevent many of the falls and associated TBIs that threaten the health of older people by taking these steps:

ENCOURAGE REGULAR EXERCISE. Exercise is the best way for older adults to reduce the risk of falling because it improves strength and balance.

MAKE THE HOME SAFER. Remove small rugs that people can trip on. Put frequently used items within easy reach so a step stool is not needed to reach them. Install grab bars in showers and tubs. Use nonstick decals or mats. Older people should wear shoes with nonslip soles at home instead of slippers and socks. Older people need more light to see well, so install better lighting and use stronger lightbulbs.

SCHEDULE A VISION EXAM. Conditions such as glaucoma and cataracts can reduce vision, increasing the risk for falls and head injuries. Be sure eyeglasses are up to date.

REVIEW MEDICATIONS. A doctor or a pharmacist should regularly review all the medications older people take. Some may increase the risk for falls. People who take blood-thinning medications (such as Coumadin or Plavix) should be seen immediately by a doctor if they hit their head. The risk of bleeding into the brain after a head injury is very high if a person is on these drugs.

CHAPTER 7

MOTOR VEHICLE ACCIDENTS

Brad Christensen was seventeen years old when he suffered a severe brain injury in a freak accident in his home state of Maryland in 2010. "I was getting into the back seat of a car and the driver started driving off. I couldn't do anything but hold on. Eventually I fell out of the car and hit my head really hard," Brad said on a brain injury survivor's blog. A helicopter took Brad to a major trauma center.

"The doctors kept me in a medically induced coma for two weeks," Brad said. "The pressure inside my brain got so high they had to remove part of my forehead so my brain could safely swell." Brad was later transferred to a rehabilitation center.

"When I woke up I was very confused and frightened. I didn't know what had happened or why I was in the hospital." Brad went home after nearly three months of rehab.

Brad later studied automotive repair at a vocational school. He still lives with challenges. He says of his life, "It's tough because I now have a horrible memory and it's difficult to concentrate. Sometimes I get really depressed. I no longer have a sense of smell and I'm deaf in one ear. I can't do anything about it, so I'm going to make lemonade out of the situation," he joked.

Motor vehicle accidents (MVAs) are the leading cause of death among people between the ages of five and thirty-four in the United States. In addition, they are the second most common cause of TBI in the United States. Brain injuries sustained in an MVA (including automobile, motorcycle, bicycle, and pedestrian accidents) are especially serious. About one-third of people who die of TBIs were injured in MVAs.

BY THE NUMBERS

Motor vehicle accidents cause about 295,000 diagnosed TBIs each year. About 11 million motor vehicle accidents are reported in the United States each year.

An estimated 2.4 million Americans are injured in those accidents.

MVAs are the leading cause of death among US teens.

It's easy to understand why brain injuries suffered in auto accidents are so serious. Think of it like this. When a person inside an auto moving at 50 miles (80 km) an hour is hit by another vehicle, the brain goes immediately from 50 miles an hour to zero. The brain slams back and forth inside the skull resulting in severe damage. MVAs cause many other types of injuries as well. Neck and back injuries are the most common, followed by brain injuries.

BICYCLES

Riding bicycles is a favorite activity among children, teenagers, and many adults. While bicycling is a lot of fun, it can also be risky. Head injuries are the most common cause of death and serious injury in bicycle crashes. Wearing a bicycle helmet is the best way to protect against these injuries. Sizing pads inside the helmet can be adjusted so that it fits snugly. Be sure the helmet you buy and wear is approved by safety organizations such as the Consumer Product Safety Commission (CPSC) or the American National Standards Institute (ANSI). And remember that the protective Styrofoam liner inside a bicycle helmet is made for a one-time use only. The helmet should be replaced after any bicycling accident involving the head because it no longer offers adequate protection in the event of a future crash.

In a study published in 2012, researchers dropped human skulls with and without helmets from various heights onto a chunk of steel. They discovered a well-fitting helmet reduced skull acceleration up to 87 percent. If the skull doesn't move so much, neither does the brain. Yet only one-fourth of all bicyclists consistently wear bicycle helmets, even though some states require it. The National Highway Traffic Safety Administration (NHTSA) estimates the use of bicycle helmets by people ages four to fifteen would prevent up to forty-five thousand head injuries per year.

CHILD PASSENGER

TBIs cause most of the deaths and injuries among children ages fourteen and under who are in MVAs each year. While it is common knowledge that child restraint systems (seat belts and car seats) can save lives, half a million children ride in vehicles without seat belts or safety seats at least part of the time. Adults who don't wear seat belts are less likely to strap in their children. In addition, the majority of people who do use child restraint systems use them incorrectly.

The US National Highway Traffic Safety Administration has found that in some areas of the country, almost 75 percent of child vehicle safety restraints were being used incorrectly. If used properly, restraint systems can dramatically reduce the risk of head injury.

Correctly used, safety seats dramatically reduce the risk of traumatic brain injury and death in children. Choosing the proper child restraint system depends on the age, height, and weight of a child. For example, infants and children through the age of two should ride in rear-facing seats in the backseat of the car. Children up to the age of four or 40 pounds (18 kg) can ride in front-facing seats in the backseat. After reaching that age or weight, children should be buckled into booster seats until they are eight years old or 57 inches (1.5 m) tall. Children can use the car's seat belt if it fits properly once they've reached that age or height. Children through the age of twelve should not sit in front seats because air bag deployment can injure or kill smaller passengers.

TEEN DRIVERS

Teens look forward to the freedoms that come with getting their driver's licenses. But the license also comes with a huge responsibility: the responsibility to drive safely without being impaired by alcohol or drugs or distracted by electronic devices.

Teens are at high risk of injury and death in MVAs for several reasons. Teens are more likely than older drivers to underestimate dangerous driving situations. They're more likely to speed and to follow other cars too closely. They also have the lowest rate of seat belt use in the United States. Some teens just don't believe that bad things can happen to them.

MVAs account for more than one-third of teen deaths. Per mile driven, teen drivers are four times more likely to crash than older drivers. And the death rate for teen boys is about twice

According to the CDC, motor vehicle crashes and traffic-related incidents result in the largest percentage of TBI-related deaths (31.8 percent) among all age groups. Texting while driving is a leading cause of such crashes.

that of teen girls. TBIs and other serious injuries also result from MVAs, bringing close to three hundred thousand teens to ERs each year.

IMPAIRED AND DISTRACTED DRIVERS

Driving while impaired by alcohol or drugs endangers everyone. Drivers, passengers, people in other cars, and pedestrians are at risk for traumatic brain injury when impaired drivers are on the road. One-third of traffic-related deaths in the United States are caused by drunk drivers. In addition, alcohol-related crashes cause injuries such as TBIs every two minutes. The majority of children who die in MVAs from TBIs and other critical injuries were riding with drivers who had been drinking.

To prevent serious injury and death caused by drunk driving, it's wise to give car keys to a designated sober driver. Another solution is for people who have been drinking to take a cab or a bus home, or to call a friend or a family member to pick them up. People should refuse to ride with a driver who's been drinking. Friends should not let friends drive drunk.

Alcohol is not the only cause of impaired driving. Driving while performing other activities can impair a person as much as alcohol. On average, eight or nine people die in distracted driving crashes each day. Countless others sustain TBIs and serious injuries. Texting while driving is the most dangerous form of distracted driving. A texting driver is twenty-three times more likely to crash than a person giving full attention to driving. Other activities, such as using cell phones, eating, or talking to passengers also distract drivers.

Like alcohol, sleepiness increases the risk of MVAs and serious injuries such as TBIs. Driving while drowsy impairs reaction time, judgment, and vision. It slows information processing in the brain and decreases alertness. Accidents caused by drowsy drivers typically involve only one vehicle. The driver is usually alone, and injuries tend to be serious or fatal.

MOTORCYCLES

The thrill of being one with the machine. The joy of communing with the scenery. The unmatched sense of freedom and adventure. There are dozens of reasons why people love their motorcycles. While most people drive responsibly and safely, driving a motorcycle can be dangerous. Motorcyclists are five times more likely to be injured per mile traveled than people in cars and trucks. And when an accident does occur, motorcyclists are twenty-five times more likely to die than passengers in car accidents.

More Americans are riding motorcycles than ever before. Yet not all states require bikers to wear helmets, even though research shows close to a 70 percent reduction in the risk of TBI among bikers who wear helmets.

Many of the serious injuries and deaths associated with motorcycle riding are due to TBIs. Wearing properly fitting helmets reduces such injuries. An analysis of sixty-one studies showed that wearing motorcycle helmets reduced TBI injuries by 69 percent and TBI deaths by 42 percent. Even though helmets dramatically reduce motorcycle-related TBIs, only nineteen states and the District of Columbia required all motorcyclists to wear helmets as of 2013. Three states have no motorcycle helmet laws, and many require helmets only for riders younger than seventeen or eighteen. Pennsylvania had a helmet law but repealed it in 2003. Within two years, deaths by TBI in that state increased 66 percent and hospitalizations for severe TBI jumped 78 percent.

The CDC reports that both the death rate and the injury rate from MVAs decreased during the ten-year period from 2001 to 2010. Safer cars, better highways, and greater use of seat belts and child restraint systems all contributed to improved safety.

CHAPTER 8

LIVING WITH TBI!

On January 8, 2011, US congresswoman Gabrielle Giffords stood on a small stage in the parking lot of a Safeway grocery store near Tucson, Arizona. The popular politician enjoyed meeting with local citizens. She called these informal meetings Congress on Your Corner. The peaceful morning went horribly wrong when a gunman in the crowd started shooting.

"I saw the congresswoman talking to two people, and then this man suddenly came up and shot her in the head," said Dr. Steven Rayle, who witnessed the shootings.

Six people died. Giffords and twelve others were injured. The bullet that hit Giffords entered the left

Representative Gabrielle Giffords and her husband (left) at an event in 2009, two years before a gunman shot her in the head. The photo at right from May 2011 clearly shows an indentation on the left side of her head. Surgeons removed a large piece of her skull in that region to allow her brain to swell safely. The piece was eventually replaced with synthetic material.

side of her skull. It traveled completely through her brain and went out the other side. In critical condition, she was airlifted to a nearby hospital. Doctors removed skull fragments and a small area of damaged brain. They next removed a sizable piece of the skull to allow her brain to swell without further injury. Doctors put Giffords into a medically induced coma to rest her brain and give it time to heal. A breathing machine pumped air into her lungs. Other machines gave her food and water. Giffords's family and friends waited at her bedside, uncertain if she would live or die.

The bullet injured the left side of Giffords's brain, which for most people controls movement on the right side of the body. Doctors and therapists began Giffords's rehabilitation early. Within days, she was sitting and standing with help. At the end of January 2012, she was transferred to a rehabilitation hospital in Houston, Texas, for intensive therapy. Giffords is making a remarkable recovery. She spoke at the US Senate's

Judiciary Committee on Gun Violence in January 2013 to promote tougher gun control laws.

Giffords resigned from the US House of Representatives in January 2012 saying she needs further rehabilitation. Yet not all brain-injured people are as fortunate as Giffords in their recovery. Giffords's mental abilities are intact. Her speech is slow but clear. She walks with a limp because her right leg is weak. Her right arm has little movement. Even with her TBI, Giffords hopes to return to public service in the future.

TBIs leave people with a wide variety of problems because different parts of the brain control different functions. Depending on the area of the brain injury, people with TBIs may not be able to move their arms and legs normally. They may not be able to think or speak clearly. Behavioral and emotional problems can occur. TBI may also cause seizures. These changes may be temporary or permanent, mild or serious. While TBIs and brain tumors can cause similar symptoms, doctors can easily tell the difference with imaging studies.

TREATMENT OF SERIOUS TBI

While most people with concussions are treated as outpatients, those with moderate to severe brain injuries require extensive medical care. Each year about 275,000 Americans are admitted to hospitals after suffering moderate and severe TBIs. This includes people with gunshot wounds to the head and people badly injured in auto accidents. Soldiers injured in explosions need hospitalization, as do people hit in the head with hard objects such as a bat or a brick.

Many TBI victims arrive at the hospital in critical condition. Medical staff must be sure patients can breathe properly.

It may be necessary to insert a breathing tube into the lungs and connect the tube to a ventilator—a machine to assist breathing. Patients with serious head injuries receive imaging studies such as CT scans and MRIs. These scans show the tissue and blood vessels inside the brain in much greater detail than X-rays do.

Emergency surgery may be needed to stop bleeding inside the brain or to remove blood clots. Foreign objects such as bullets, shrapnel, or skull fragments must be removed if it is possible to do so safely. If medications cannot stop the brain from swelling, surgeons will take out a piece

BY THE NUMBERS

Traumatic brain injuries kill about 52,000 Americans each year.

TBIs disable about 90,000 Americans annually.

An estimated 5.3 million Americans are living with disabilities related to TBI.

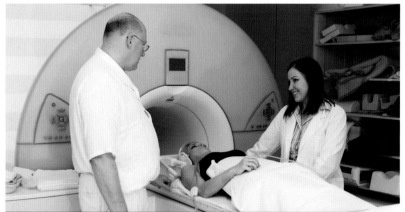

Magnetic resonance imaging (MRI) can be a useful tool in diagnosing TBI. However, military personnel exposed to blasts often have symptoms of brain injury that are hard to detect. For this reason, researchers are studying a supersensitive MRI technique called diffusion tensor imaging, which can detect signs of injury that are too subtle for standard imaging.

of the skull to allow room for the injured brain to swell outside the skull, as they did for Giffords. Surgeons later replaced the missing section of her skull with a piece of plastic that was shaped, by computer, to match the shape of the lost bone. Tiny titanium screws hold the plastic to the skull.

Many medications are used to treat head injury. TBI patients may need intravenous fluids if they cannot eat or drink by themselves. Important minerals such as sodium, potassium, and calcium may be added to intravenous fluids. Medications may be required to stabilize blood pressure. Whenever an object breaks through the protective skull, bacteria can enter the brain and cause serious infections. If the patient had a penetrating head injury, antibiotics—medications that kill bacteria—are given.

Patients may be in a coma after a brain injury. People in comas are so deeply unconscious they cannot respond to anything. A comatose patient has no voluntary movement, no response to pain, and may lose all reflexes such as swallowing and blinking. Sometimes doctors use strong medications to put patients into medically induced comas.

People may die of complications from severe TBIs or wake up completely healed, depending on what part of the brain is injured. The usual outcome is somewhere in between. A few patients survive, only to remain in a vegetative state. In this condition, the eyes are open, but no true consciousness or thinking process is present. Other patients suffer varying degrees of lifelong disability because of their TBIs. Disabilities include problems with walking, talking, thinking, and performing everyday activities such as getting dressed. However, early intensive rehabilitation can often produce significant results.

THE INJURED BRAIN

Left brain injury can cause these conditions:
- difficulty speaking or understanding the meaning of words
- memory problems
- emotional issues such as depression and anxiety
- weakness of the right side of the body

Right brain injury can cause these conditions:
- altered creativity and deficit in music perception
- visual-spatial impairment
- memory problems
- weakness of the left side of the body

Injuries scattered through both sides of the brain can cause these conditions:
- confusion
- slower thinking
- reduced attention and concentration
- impaired cognitive skills in all areas

REHABILITATING THE TRAUMATIZED BRAIN

The brain has an amazing ability to repair itself. During the healing process, the brain reorganizes to compensate for injuries. Undamaged axons sprout new connections to reconnect neurons severed by injury. New nerve pathways form so the brain can better complete its important jobs. If one part of the brain is damaged, another part may take over some of its functions.

Rehabilitation is the process of giving patients the treatment they need to help them recover. The goal of rehabilitation is to return patients to normal or as near normal as possible. No one can say for sure how much a particular patient will improve. With TBIs, most improvement occurs during the first year after injury.

Rehabilitation usually starts immediately after the injury, even if the patient is in a coma. Physical therapists exercise the patient's arms and legs to preserve muscle function. It's important to get patients sitting and standing even if they can't do it alone. Nova Sbrusch is one of the physical therapists who worked with Gabrielle Giffords at TIRR Memorial Herman Hospital in Houston. "By getting patients standing and moving early, they will be more alert," she says. "We want to stimulate their reticular activating system [the part of the brain that

A patient at a Boston rehabilitation clinic works with a therapist to learn to walk again. The patient almost died from a TBI suffered in a car crash that killed several other people.

controls wakefulness]. It's hard to get someone's attention and keep it when they're lying down."

Rehab hospitals have specialized teams that include doctors, nurses, and therapists. Physical therapists help patients improve their movement so they can sit, stand, and walk. Occupational therapists assist patients to relearn everyday activities such as eating and dressing. Speech therapists help patients regain their speech. Psychologists who specialize in brain injury help patients with problems such as depression and anger. Even with the best rehabilitation, TBIs leave thousands of Americans with permanent disabilities each year.

THE FUTURE OF TBI

Research into better ways to prevent and treat traumatic brain injuries has increased in recent years. One reason is the large number of soldiers suffering TBIs in Iraq and Afghanistan. In the past, many of those injuries would have been fatal. Due to improved protective gear and better medical care, more soldiers are surviving brain injuries and returning home. Also, mounting evidence shows that repeated concussions—even seemingly mild concussions—can cause permanent brain damage among athletes. This too has spurred TBI research. Three main areas of progress are technology, testing, and treatment.

In 2012 the US Army and the NFL joined forces to study TBI in soldiers and football players. When it comes to the injured brain, football players and service members have a lot in common. The two organizations share research into the cause, treatment, and prevention of TBI. In one study, seven thousand soldiers were deployed with sensors in their helmets to record concussive events to help doctors better understand how TBIs affect the brain. The NFL is planning to do the same for its players.

Explosive blasts can damage the brain even when shrapnel or other objects don't hit the head. A military medical research division has invented a blast explosion meter small enough to be worn on a protective vest during combat missions. The meter records the force of any blast and radios the information to camp. This helps doctors evaluate potential brain injuries and begin treatment earlier.

The US Army is also trying out an Automated Binocular Vision Tester. Often soldiers suffering from blast injuries have problems with eye movement and focus. With the tester, an injured soldier can peer into the binoculars for a quick vision test, allowing for early treatment if necessary.

A new mouth guard is being developed for athletes in sports such as basketball and soccer, where helmets are not worn. The guard can sense and record head impacts. This information allows researchers to further study head impacts in which players do not wear protective headgear.

Another group of researchers has invented a tiny sensor that reads brain activity by measuring changes in the brain's magnetic field. Scientists want to make the sugar-cube-sized device small

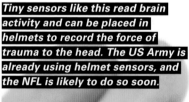
Tiny sensors like this read brain activity and can be placed in helmets to record the force of trauma to the head. The US Army is already using helmet sensors, and the NFL is likely to do so soon.

enough to place into helmets and headgear worn by football players and boxers. This would allow athletes to be pulled from the game at the first sign of head trauma.

BETTER TESTS AND TREATMENTS

Injured hearts release chemicals into the blood that doctors test to see if patients have had a heart attack. Researchers are working to find out if the injured brain does the same thing. If it does and if a blood test can be developed, it would mean earlier identification and treatment of TBI.

In 2013 scientists announced an important new way to identify abnormal tau protein deposits in the brain. In a small study, researchers injected a chemical into the bloodstream. The chemical attaches to tau protein deposits, making them visible in a type of brain scanner called a positron-emission tomography (PET) scan. With further development, the test may be the first way to identify CTE and Alzheimer's in a living brain.

The US Army is also working to develop a pill that soldiers could take before entering battle. The experimental pill, called NNZ-2566, would help protect brain cells if an injury occurs.

In another development, researchers are using nanoparticles to help restore blood flow to badly injured brains. (A nanoparticle is a bit of matter so small that it takes a thousand of them to equal the width of a human hair.) Increased blood flow would speed recovery of the concussed brain.

Anyone can suffer a traumatic brain injury. Just ask former police officer Teri McKown. She was on her way to work one morning on a crowded freeway in Southern California.

TBI AFFECTS THE ENTIRE FAMILY

When patients are discharged home following a TBI, their care often falls to family members. Caregivers of people who have suffered a TBI may experience feelings of distress, anxiety, anger, and depression. They may feel overwhelmed and frustrated with the responsibility of caring for someone who has changed forever. Experts recommend that family members do the following:

- Be involved in the rehabilitation process from the beginning.
- Modify the home as necessary to meet the patient's needs.
- Establish a schedule with as much activity as the patient can tolerate.
- Structure the patient's time and surroundings. Consistency is reassuring to a person who may suffer from memory problems.
- Seek help from other family members, friends, and health-care professionals, especially during periods of stress or fatigue.
- Get support. Many hospitals, communities, and organizations offer support groups for caregivers. Sharing problems and solutions can ease the isolation that caregivers may feel.

McKown remembers that, "The car next to me spun out of control and whacked my car. [It] rolled onto the passenger side and skidded across the pavement shooting up sparks. I was afraid the car would catch fire. A second later, my car rolled over four times. If I hadn't been wearing my seat belt, I would have been ejected through the windshield and probably would have died."

Paramedics took McKown to a small local hospital. Doctors said she didn't have a concussion and discharged her. "I was staggering like a drunk when I left the hospital with my parents." She was unable to return to her former job with the police department.

Despite several years of suffering from memory loss, poor concentration, and fatigue, McKown couldn't get the help she needed. "I felt like I was dead inside." Finally, a psychiatrist—a medical doctor who specializes in treating mental disorders—was able to help. McKown quickly improved, with medications to regulate her brain chemistry, counseling, and a support group.

"Don't be afraid to tell someone how you're feeling," McKown says. "I might have recovered more quickly if I'd received the proper treatment earlier. Just because you look okay, doesn't mean you are okay. Get the help you need. Never give up."

Each person is responsible for the care and feeding of his or her own brain. Feed it well by living a healthy lifestyle. Care for it well by avoiding risky situations that could result in a brain injury. Remember, only one brain to a customer.

Alzheimer's disease: a brain disease that causes progressive loss of memory, thinking, and language skills leading to dementia, inability to function, and death

chronic traumatic encephalopathy (CTE): a progressive degenerative brain disease seen in people with a history of repeated head trauma. CTE has been found in athletes such as football players and boxers and in military service personnel exposed to blast injuries. Currently, it can only be diagnosed after death.

closed head injury: a traumatic brain injury in which the head strikes a hard object or is struck by a hard object, leaving the skull intact. This type of injury can occur on the playing field, in combat, in a motor vehicle accident, or in accidents at home.

cognitive: referring to higher-level mental skills such as thinking, making decisions, reasoning, memory, and judgment

coma: a deep state of unconsciousness in which a person cannot move, think, see, or speak

concussion: a milder form of traumatic brain injury in which the brain moves inside the skull due to an external force such as a helmet hit or an explosion

CT scan: this procedure creates a series of cross-sectional X-rays of the head and brain. CT stands for "computed tomography."

dementia: a brain disorder involving the deterioration of mental processes such as memory, thinking, and judgment. Dementia is associated with TBIs and diseases such as Alzheimer's.

depression: a mental condition characterized by extreme sadness and hopelessness. Depression may be associated with TBIs.

improvised explosive device (IED): a homemade bomb. IEDs are common in the war zones of Iraq and Afghanistan and have caused a large number of TBIs among military personnel.

MRI (magnetic resonance imaging): a scan that uses the body's magnetic fields to detect changes in tissues and blood vessels. MRIs are one way to detect TBIs.

penetrating head injury: a traumatic brain injury in which an object such as a bullet or a piece of shrapnel pierces the skull and enters the brain

post-concussion syndrome: a condition in which concussion symptoms last for many weeks or months

post-traumatic stress disorder (PTSD): a mental health condition triggered by a terrifying event. The condition can include flashbacks, nightmares, and severe anxiety.

rehabilitation: treatment to help patients recover from a disease or a serious condition. A program of rehabilitation may include physical and speech therapy. The goal is to return patients to normal or as near normal as possible.

second impact syndrome: a rare but potentially fatal condition that occurs when a person suffers a second concussion before fully recovering from the first

seizure: a sudden disruption of the brain's normal electrical activity that may be accompanied by changes in consciousness and repetitive muscle jerking

tau protein: abnormal proteins found in the brains of people with chronic traumatic encephalopathy and Alzheimer's disease

traumatic brain injury (TBI): this term refers to injuries to the brain caused by blows to the head or by objects such as bullets penetrating the skull. TBIs may range from mild concussions to comas and death.

vegetative state: a condition in which patients are unconscious and unaware of their surroundings but appear to have periods of wakefulness

5 Jeremiah Oshan, "Concussions Force New England Revolution's Taylor Twellman into Retirement," SB*Nation, November 3, 2010, http://www.sbnation.com/soccer/2010/11/3/1792552/concussions-force-new-england-revolutions-taylor-twellman-into.

6 Ibid.

11 US Department of Health and Human Services, Centers for Disease Control and Prevention, "All Concussions Are Serious," cdc.gov, last modified June 2010, http://www.cdc.gov/concussion/pdf/Main_Message_Poster-a.pdf.

12 Gina DiGravio and Kristin Pressly, "Boston University Researchers Report NHL Player Derek Boogaard Had Evidence of Early Chronic Traumatic Encephalopathy," BU Center for the Study of Traumatic Encephalopathy, last modified December 6, 2011, http://www.bu.edu/cste/news/press-releases/december-6-2011/.

14 Ron Kroichick, "Trying to Protect Vulnerable Pitchers," sfgate.com, November 6, 2012, http://www.sfgate.com/preps/article/Trying-to-protect-vulnerable-pitchers-4010947.php#page-1.

21 Nadia Kounang, "Brain Bank Examines Athletes' Hard Hits," CNN Health, February 27, 2012, http://www.cnn.com/2012/01/27/health/big-hits-broken-dreams-brain-bank/index.html.

21 Ibid.

24 Kate Snow, Sarah Koch, Deirdre Cohen, and Jessica Hopper, "Concussion Crisis Growing in Girls' Soccer," Rock Center with Brian Williams, May 9, 2012, http://rockcenter.nbcnews.com/_news/2012/05/09/11604307-concussion-crisis-growing-in-girls-soccer?lite.

25 Ibid.

25 Ibid.

27 Ibid.

29–30 Lori McGowan, interview by author, September 5, 2012.

30 Lori McGowan, "Girls' LAX; A Referee's View, Written by Dr. Lori McGowan, Biology Professor, Lacrosse Referee," SportsConcussions.org, last modified June 25, 2012, http://sportsconcussions.tumblr.com/post/25895613828/girls-lax-referees-view-written-by-dr-lori-.

30 McGowan, interview by author.

31 Cari Nierenberg, "College Football Players' Concussion Rates Double," WebMD Health News, July 12, 2012, http://www.webmd.com/fitness-exercise/news/20120712/college-football-players-concussion-rates-double.

31 Denise Mann, "Surge Seen in Concussions among College Football Players," Health Day Daily Newsfeed, July 12, 2012, http://www.health-quest.org/body.cfm?id=385&action=detail&ref=42443.

33 Associated Press, "Study Finds Seau Had Brain Disease," Wall Street Journal, January 10, 2013, http://online.wsj.com/article/SB10001424127887324081704578233690706118144.html.

35 Kevin Allen, "Costly Concussions Continue to Confound NHL," USA Today Sports, January 24, 2012, http://usatoday30.usatoday.com/sports/hockey/nhl/story/2012-01-23/costly-concussions/52762290/1.

35 Ibid.

36 Associated Press, "Panel: Helmets Reduce, Not Eliminate, Concussions," Bloomberg

Businessweek, June 21, 2011, http://www.businessweek.com/ap/financialnews/D9O0C6G00.htm.

37 Associated Press, "QB Quinn Admits Trying to Play through Concussion," *News-PressNow.com*, November 7, 2012, http://www.newspressnow.com/sports/professional/national_football_league/kansas_city_chiefs/article_008fa2a8-bf02-52e3-a89e-f2819ec5b5d0.html.

38 Ibid.

50 Mark Thompson, "Battling PTSD and TBI," *Time U.S.: Military Mental Health*, September 11, 2012,. http://nation.time.com/2012/09/11/battling-ptsd-and-tbi/#ixzz26Cljw87a.

51 Marcia Henry, interview by author, September 14, 2012.

51–52 Ibid.

52 Ibid.

58 Brad Christensen, "Personal Stories," Brain Injury Association of America, last modified February 16, 2012, http://www.biausa.org/_blog/Personal_Stories/post/Brad_Christensen/21.

58–59 Ibid.

59 Ibid.

66 Marc Lacey and David M. Herszenhorn, "In Attack's Wake, Political Repercussions," *New York Times*, January 8, 2011, http://www.nytimes.com/2011/01/09/us/politics/09giffords.html?pagewanted=all&_r=0.

72–73 Marcia Frellick, "Head Start," *TodayinPT.com*, April 11, 2011, http://news.todayinpt.com/article/20110411/TODAYINPT0104/110408007.

77 Teri McKown, interview by author, November 14, 2012.

77 Ibid.

77 Ibid.

SELECTED BIBLIOGRAPHY

Boston University Center for the Study of Traumatic Encephalopathy. "Game Changers." CST video. YouTube. 5:20. Accessed December 8, 2012. http://www.bu.edu/cste/.

———. "VA CSTE Brain Bank." BU Center for the Study of Traumatic Encephalopathy. Accessed December 8, 2012. http://www.bu.edu/cste/our-research/brain-bank/

———. "What Is CTE?" Accessed December 8, 2012. http://www.bu.edu/cste/about/what-is-cte/

Brain Injury Association of America. "Living with Brain Injury." Accessed December 9, 2012. http://www.biausa.org/living-with-brain-injury.htm.

Brainlinemilitary. "Blast Injuries and the Brain." Accessed December 9, 2012. http://www.brainlinemilitary.org/content/2010/12/blast-injuries-and-the-brain.html.

Carroll, Linda, and David Rosner. *The Concussion Crisis*. New York: Simon & Schuster, 2011.

Centers for Disease Control and Prevention. "Falls among Older Adults." Last modified September 20, 2012. http://www.cdc.gov/homeandrecreationalsafety/Falls/adultfalls.html.

———. "Kids and Teens." Last modified May 16, 2012. http://www.cdc.gov/TraumaticBrainInjury/kids_teens.html.

———. "Impaired Driving: Get the Facts." Last modified October 2, 2012. http://www.cdc.gov/Motorvehiclesafety/Impaired_Driving/impaired-drv_factsheet.html.

———. "Motor Vehicle Safety." Last modified October 3, 2012. http://www.cdc.gov/motorvehiclesafety/index.html.

———. "Severe Traumatic Brain Injury." Last modified September 21, 2012. http://www.cdc.gov/TraumaticBrainInjury/severe.html.

———. "Teen Drivers Fact Sheet." Last modified October 2, 2012. http://www.cdc.gov/Motorvehiclesafety/teen_drivers/teendrivers_factsheet.html.

———. "Traumatic Brain Injury in the United States: Emergency Department Visits, Hospitalizations and Deaths 2002–2006." Last modified March 2010. http://www.cdc.gov/traumaticbraininjury/pdf/blue_book.pdf.

———. "What Are the Leading Causes of TBI?" Last modified June 15, 2010. http://www.cdc.gov/TraumaticBrainInjury/causes.html.

———. "What Are the Signs and Symptoms of Concussion?" Last modified March 8, 2010. http://www.cdc.gov/concussion/signs_symptoms.html.

Frommer, Leah J., Kelly K. Gurka, Kevin M. Cross, Christopher D. Ingersoll, R. Dawn Comstock, and Susan A. Saliba. "Sex Differences in Concussion Symptoms of High School Athletes." *Journal of Athletic Training* 46, no. 1 (2011): 76–84.

Gregory, Sean. "The Problem with Football." *Time,* January 28, 2010. http://www.time.com/time/magazine/article/0,9171,1957459-1,00.html.

Halstead M. E., K. D. Walter, and the Council on Sports Medicine and Fitness. "Clinical Report: Sport-Related Concussion in Children and Adolescents." *Pediatrics* 126, no. 3 (2010): 597–614.

Joseph, R. *Head Injury & Brain Damage.* Cambridge: Cambridge University Press, 2011.

Lincoln, Andrew. E, Shane V. Caswell, Jon L. Almquist, Reginald E. Dunn, Joseph B. Norris, and Richard Y. Hinton. "Trends in Concussion Incidence in High School Sports." *American Journal of Sports Medicine* 39, no. 5 (2011): 958–963.

NBC. "Contact Sport: Should Heading Be Banned from Youth Soccer?" *Rock Center with Brian Williams.* NBC video. 0:30. May 9, 2012. http://video.msnbc.msn.com/rock-center/47364254#47364254.

North American Brain Injury Society. "Brain Injury Facts." Accessed December 8, 2012. http://www.nabis.org/brain-injury-facts/.

Summerall, E. Lanier. "Traumatic Brain Injury and PTSD." National Center for PTSD. Last modified December 20, 2011. http://www.ptsd.va.gov/professional/pages/traumatic-brain-injury-ptsd.asp.

US Department of Defense. "Defense and Veterans Brain Injury Center." Accessed December 9, 2012. http://www.dvbic.org/audience/service-members-veterans.

———. "Numbers for Traumatic Brain Injury Worldwide Totals." Last modified May 16, 2012. http://www.dvbic.org/sites/default/files/uploads/dod-tbi-2000-2012.pdf.

———. "Worldwide Numbers for Traumatic Brain Injury." Last modified August 20, 2012. http://www.health.mil/Research/TBI_Numbers.aspx.

US Department of Transportation. "2010 Motor Vehicle Crashes." Last modified February 2012. http://www-nrd.nhtsa.dot.gov/Pubs/811552.pdf.

FOR FURTHER INFORMATION

BOOKS

Bouvard, Marguerite G. *Invisible Wounds of War: Coming Home from Iraq and Afghanistan.* New York: Prometheus Books, 2012.

Cantu, Robert, and Mark Hyman. *Concussions and Our Kids.* New York: Houghton Mifflin Harcourt, 2012.

Carroll, Linda, and David Rosner. *The Concussion Crisis.* New York: Simon & Schuster, 2011.

Kamberg, Mary-Lane. *Headlines! Sports Concussions.* New York: Rosen Publishing, 2011.

Marcovitz, Hal. *Diseases & Disorders: Brain Trauma.* Farmington Hills, MI: Lucent Books, 2009.

Mason, Michael Paul. *Head Cases: Stories of Brain Injury and Its Aftermath.* New York: Farrar, Straus and Giroux, 2009.

McClafferty, Carla Killough. *Fourth Down and Inches: Concussions and Football's Make-or-Break Moment.* Minneapolis: Carolrhoda Books, 2013.

ORGANIZATIONS AND WEBSITES

American College of Sports Medicine (ACSM)
http://www.acsm.org/
ACSM is the world's largest sports medicine and exercise science organization. ACSM is dedicated to advancing scientific research to provide educational and practical applications of exercise science and sports medicine. ACSM promotes and integrates scientific research, education and practical applications of sports medicine and exercise science to maintain and enhance physical performance, fitness, health, and quality of life.

Boston University Center for the Study of Traumatic Encephalopathy (CSTE)
http://www.bu.edu/cste/
The CSTE is a joint venture between Boston University School of Medicine and Sports Legacy Institute. Its mission is to conduct research on chronic traumatic encephalopathy through the study of its neuropathology, pathogenesis, clinical presentation, disease course, and genetic and environmental risk factors, and to find ways to prevent this progressive dementia. The CSTE collects the donated brains of deceased athletes and others with a history of repeated concussions.

Brain Injury Association of America
http://www.biausa.org
The Brain Injury Association of America is the country's oldest and largest nationwide brain injury advocacy organization. Its mission is to be the voice of brain injury. Through advocacy, education, and research, the association brings help, hope, and healing to millions of individuals living with brain injury. The site has extensive information for family and caregivers.

Centers for Disease Control and Prevention Traumatic Brain Injury Center
http://www.cdc.gov/TraumaticBrainInjury/
The CDC's mission is to promote health and quality of life by preventing and controlling disease, injury, and disability. The CDC monitors and investigates

health problems around the world and in the United States. Its website offers extensive information about traumatic brain injury for all age groups and sports, and includes a variety of interactive media including podcasts and video clips. The site provides information and resources for family and caregivers.

Defense and Veterans Brain Injury Center
http://www.dvbic.org/
The Defense and Veterans Brain Injury Center is a part of the US military health system. Its mission is to serve active duty military, their beneficiaries, and veterans with traumatic brain injuries through state-of-the-art clinical care, innovative clinical research initiatives and educational programs, and support for force health protection services.

Distracted Driving: US Department of Transportation National Highway Traffic Safety Administration
http://www.distraction.gov/
This US government website is committed to raising awareness and providing information to people who are interested in decreasing the thousands of auto accidents that occur each year involving distracted drivers. The site wants people to get involved in their communities and help to make roads safer for all Americans.

Drowsy Driving.org
http://drowsydriving.org/about/
This site is part of the National Sleep Foundation, an educational and scientific organization dedicated to improving sleep health and safety through education, public awareness, and advocacy. The drowsy driving site is dedicated to the prevention of drowsy driving. The foundation conducts studies and provides information to help stop the one hundred thousand automobile crashes per year attributed to driving drowsy.

North American Brain Injury Society
http://www.nabis.org/
The North American Brain Injury Society is comprised of professional members involved in the care or issues surrounding brain injury. The principal mission of the organization is moving brain injury science into practice. The organization was created specifically to address the needs of multidisciplinary professionals dedicated to brain injury. The society provides education programs, scientific updates, and a platform for communication and professional exchange.

Sports Legacy Institute
http://sportslegacy.org/
The mission of the Sports Legacy Institute is to advance the study, treatment, and prevention of the effects of brain trauma in athletes and other at-risk groups. The institute is dedicated to solving the concussion crisis in sports and the military. The institute makes sports safer through educational programs, policy development, and increasing awareness of concussions through the media.

American Foundation for Suicide Prevention (AFSP)
https://www.afsp.org/
AFSP is the leading national not-for-profit organization exclusively dedicated to understanding and preventing suicide through research, education, and advocacy and to reaching out to people with mental disorders and those impacted by suicide. It funds research, provides educational programs to the public and health-care professionals, and resources for at-risk individuals and families.

National Suicide Prevention Lifeline
(800) 273-8255
http://www.suicidepreventionlifeline.org/
The suicide prevention lifeline provides a list of suicide warning signs and educational resources. The phone is staffed twenty-four hours a day in English and Spanish and offers an option specifically for veterans.

VIDEOS

"Gunnar Sandberg 5 & Marin Catholic Baseball"
http://www.youtube.com/watch?v=-Qw0hwE019w
Gunnar Sandberg's teammates talk about his TBI following a baseball hit to the head.

"Inside Shock Trauma: A Teen's Survival Story"
http://www.youtube.com/watch?v=InM48hawL2Y&feature=related
Corey Ragan, seventeen years old, talks about the TBI he suffered while driving drunk.

"Personal Journeys: Scott Lilley"
http://www.traumaticbraininjuryatoz.org/Personal-Journeys/Personal-Journeys/Scott-Lilley
Scott Lilley and his parents talk about his TBI following an EID in Iraq.

"Worthington Woman Shot by Man Is an Inspiration"
http://www.youtube.com/watch?v=zmj2x2kyVdA
Rachel Barezinsky talks about her TBI following a gunshot wound to the head.

LERNER
SOURCE™

Expand learning beyond the printed book. Download free, complementary educational resources for this book from our website, www.lerneresource.com.

ABOUT THE AUTHOR

Connie Goldsmith is a registered nurse with a bachelor of science degree in nursing and a master of public administration degree in health care. In addition to writing fourteen nonfiction books for middle school and upper-grade readers, she has also published more than two hundred magazine articles, mostly on health topics for adults and children. Goldsmith writes a children's book review column and a child health column for a regional parenting magazine in Sacramento, California, where she lives. She has written for nurses and parents about concussions.

PHOTO ACKNOWLEDGMENTS

The images in this book are used with the permission of: © Gualtiero Boffi/Bigstock .com (xray); © Oleg Golovnev/Bigstock.com, (cracked glass) © Jim Rogash/Stringer/Getty Images, p. 5; © Laura Westlund/Independent Picture Service, pp. 6, 8, 15, 17, 40; © Stan Grossfeld/The Boston Globe via Getty Images, p. 11; Jim McIsaac/MCT/Newscom, p. 12; AP Photo/Eric Risberg, p. 14; © Collection of Jack and Beverly Wilgus, p. 23 (right); AP Photo/ Harvard Medical School, p. 23 (left); © Mike Kemp/Blend Images/Getty Images, p. 25; © Jonathan Ferrery/Getty Images, p. 28; AP Photo/The Dallas Morning News, Michael Ainsworth, p. 29; © Michael Chang/Getty Images, p. 32; © Justin K. Aller/Getty Images, p. 34; AP Photo/Ed Zurga, p. 38; AP Photo/Robert E. Klien, p. 39; Jim Mahoney/The Dallas Morning News, p. 45; © Andy Cross/The Denver Post via Getty Images, p. 49; © Michael Svoboda/Vetta/Getty Images, p. 53; © Daniel Grill/Getty Images, p. 61; © Joseph Silva Photography/Alamy, p. 62; © Comstock/Thinkstock, p. 64; © Dave Rossman/ZUMA Press/ CORBIS, p. 67 (left); P.K. Weis/AFP/Getty Images/Newscom, p. 67 (right); © Bojan Fatur/E+/ Getty Images, p. 69; AP Photo/Steven Senne, p. 72; Knappe/NIST, p. 74.

Front Cover: © Gualtiero Boffi/Bigstock.com (xray); © Oleg Golovnev/Bigstock.com, (cracked glass). Back Cover: © Oleg Golovnev/Bigstock.com. Jacket Flaps: © Oleg Golovnev/Bigstock.com.

Main body text set in Caecilia LT Std 10/15.
Typeface provided by Adobe Systems.